Write It Right

Writing a Fairy Tale

By Cecilia Minden and Kate Roth

Published in the United States of America by
CHERRY LAKE PRESS
Ann Arbor, Michigan, 2395 South Huron Parkway, Suite 200
www.cherrylakepublishing.com

Reading Adviser: Marla Conn, MS, Ed., Literacy specialist, Read-Ability, Inc.
Book Designer: Felicia Macheske
Character Illustrator: Carol Herring

Photo Credits: © Oleg Voronische/Shutterstock.com, 7; © Victoria Kovelina/Shutterstock.com, 9; © arrowsmith2/Shutterstock.com, 11; © s4svisuals/Shutterstock.com, 13; © Menno Schaefer/Shutterstock.com, 15; © myboys.me/Shutterstock.com, 21

Graphics Throughout: © simple surface/Shutterstock.com; © Mix3r/Shutterstock.com; © Artefficient/Shutterstock.com; © lemony/Shutterstock.com; © Svetolk/Shutterstock.com; © EV-DA/Shutterstock.com; © briddy/Shutterstock.com; © IreneArt/Shutterstock.com

Library of Congress Cataloging-in-Publication Data

Names: Minden, Cecilia, author. | Roth, Kate, author. | Herring, Carol, illustrator.
Title: Writing a fairy tale / by Cecilia Minden and Kate Roth ; illustrated by Carol Herring.
Description: Ann Arbor, Michigan : Cherry Lake Publishing, 2020. | Series: Write it right | Includes bibliographical references and index. | Audience: Grades 2-3
Identifiers: LCCN 2019033293 | ISBN 9781534159013 (hardcover) | ISBN 9781534161313 (paperback) | ISBN 9781534160163 (pdf) | ISBN 9781534162464 (ebook)
Subjects: LCSH: Fairy tales—Authorship—Juvenile literature.
Classification: LCC PN3377.5.F32 M563 2020 | DDC 808.06—dc23
LC record available at https://lccn.loc.gov/2019033293

Cherry Lake Publishing would like to acknowledge the work of the Partnership for 21st Century Learning, a Network of Battelle for Kids. Please visit *www.battelleforkids.org/networks/p21* for more information.

Printed in the United States of America
Corporate Graphics

CHERRY LAKE PRESS

Table of
CONTENTS

CHAPTER ONE
Once Upon a Time 4

CHAPTER TWO
Choosing Characters 8

CHAPTER THREE
Creating Conflict 12

CHAPTER FOUR
Making a Solution 16

CHAPTER FIVE
The End 18

CHAPTER SIX
Happily Ever After 20

GLOSSARY 22
FOR MORE INFORMATION 23
INDEX 24
ABOUT THE AUTHORS 24

Once Upon a Time

Fairy tales are **fantasies**. These make-believe stories often have unusual creatures like giants or witches in them. They usually begin with the words "Once upon a time."

Characters can have magical powers. For example, animals might talk or people might make things change shape. Fairy tales tell stories of good against **evil**. Good usually wins.

Fairy tales are fun to write because you can use your **imagination** to create a whole new world. Are you ready to give it a try?

One of the first things you must decide is the fairy tale's **setting**. Maybe you want your fairy tale to take place on an old bridge or at a county fair. It might be in a castle or a cottage in the forest.

Here's what you'll need to complete the activities in this book:

- Pencil
- Paper

Animals don't really talk, but in a fairy tale they can.

ACTIVITY

Choose Your Setting

INSTRUCTIONS:

1. Write the title "Planning Sheet" on the top of your paper. You will be planning your story on this paper.
2. Make a list of places for your fairy tale.
3. Be sure the places are magical.
4. Choose one place from your list for the setting of your story.

Sample Planning Sheet

SETTING IDEAS

- Beautiful castle
- Witch's cottage
- Dragon's den
- Fairy village ✓

A fairy tale may include a castle, a forest, or anywhere your imagination takes you.

CHAPTER TWO

Choosing Characters

Next, you will add your characters. You must have both good and evil characters. You can use humans or animals. You could also use fantasy characters. Elves, fairies, and dragons often appear in fairy tales. You can combine two kinds of characters to make a new one. For example, you could write about a horse with wings.

Picture your characters in your mind. What do they look like? What are their names? Do they have magical powers? What do we know about them? You will also include **dialogue**. Think about how your characters sound when they talk.

Create characters that will interest your readers.

ACTIVITY

Choose Your Characters

INSTRUCTIONS:

1. Choose characters for your fairy tale.
2. Write a list of your characters on your Planning Sheet.
3. Describe each character. How do they look? How do they sound when they speak? Are they good or evil? A hero or a **villain**? Do they have magical powers?

Sample Planning Sheet

CHARACTER IDEAS

- Lavender, the Fairy Queen
- Violet, the Fairy Princess
- Felix the Fox, a greedy villain
- Ella the Brave, a knight

ACTIVITY

Begin your story

INSTRUCTIONS:

1. Write a title for your fairy tale on a fresh sheet of paper. This is your story sheet.
2. Write the beginning of your story. Start with the words "Once upon a time."
3. Write a few sentences that describe your setting and your characters.
4. Include some dialogue. This will help your readers better understand your characters' personalities.

Sample Story Beginning

ELLA THE BRAVE SAVES THE DAY

Once upon a time, in a beautiful meadow, there was a small kingdom of fairies living among the flowers and bushes. The ruler of the fairy kingdom was Queen Lavender. She was a beautiful queen who loved all the fairies.

Queen Lavender's daughter was Princess Violet. Violet was sweet and kind. She helped her mother keep all the fairies safe from harm.

One day, Queen Lavender received word that Princess Violet had been taken and needed help. The queen called upon her bravest knight, Ella, to bring Princess Violet home. The queen gave the knight a magic bag. It had everything she needed inside it. The knight set off with the magic bag to find Princess Violet.

CHAPTER THREE

Creating Conflict

Now it is time to put the characters in **conflict** with each other. The evil character wants the good character to do something that causes harm. Your main characters will have to **outsmart** the villain.

Fairy tales often use the number three, as in three wishes or three tries to do something.

Think of different ways your characters will be in conflict. What does the villain want the hero to do? How can the hero stop the villain?

ACTIVITY

Choose Your Conflict

INSTRUCTIONS:

1. Write the word "Conflict" on your Planning Sheet.
2. Write a sentence or two about what the conflict will be. Think about how the villain wants to harm the hero.
3. Add to your story on your story sheet.

Sample Planning Sheet

CONFLICT

- Felix the Fox has captured Princess Violet. He won't let her go until the knight completes three tasks.

Sample Story Conflict

The knight came to Felix the Fox's den. She called out, "Princess Violet, it is Ella the Brave! I've come to take you back home."

Out jumped Felix the Fox!

The knight was not afraid. "Where is the princess?" she demanded.

"Violet is safe for now," said Felix. "If you want to keep her safe, you must complete three tasks."

The knight knew that Felix was tricky, but she had to save the princess. "What are the three tasks?"

Felix sneered, "First, you will sprinkle me with fairy dust so I can fly over land to find many small animals to eat. Next, I want a great cape so everyone can see how powerful I am. Finally, I know fairies collect honey from the flowers. I want a big jar of honey. Now be quick about it. I don't like waiting!"

What will the knight do?

In some stories, villains can become heroes.

CHAPTER FOUR

Making a Solution

It's time to write your **solution**. You solve the conflict between good and bad. Some fairy tales use tricks. Use your imagination!

ACTIVITY

Choose the Solution

INSTRUCTIONS:

1. Write the word "Solution" on your Planning Sheet.
2. Plan the solution to the conflict. How will the hero win out over the villain?
3. Add to your story on your story sheet.

Sample Planning Sheet

SOLUTION

- The knight gives Felix the Fox everything he asked for, but it is not what he expected.

Sample Story Solution

The knight had to think fast. She remembered that the queen gave her a magic bag with everything she needed. She opened her bag and got an idea.

“First, I will cover you with fairy dust,” said the knight. She pulled a handful of dirt from her bag and tossed it all over the fox.

“What is this?” he roared.

“The fairy castle was cleaned this morning,” said the knight. “That is the dust that was collected. So therefore, it is fairy dust. Isn’t that what you asked for?”

The fox growled as he brushed off the dirt. “Now the cape,” he said.

The knight pulled a heavy cloak from her magical bag.

“That is more like it,” said the fox. He grabbed the cloak and pulled it around his shoulders. But it was so heavy, he couldn’t stand up. “This isn’t working,” he cried. He crawled out from under the heavy cloak.

“Oh, dear,” said the knight. “Well, we will move on to the third request: a big jar of honey.” She reached once more into her magic bag and pulled out the biggest jar of honey Felix had ever seen.

“Now that is more like it,” he said. He reached up to remove the lid, but the weight of the jar landed on the fox and knocked him out.

CHAPTER FIVE

The End

The ending to your fairy tale can be short. You want the readers to know what happened. Fairy tales often have a **moral** to the story. What is the lesson we learn from your fairy tale?

ACTIVITY

Choose the Ending

INSTRUCTIONS:

1. Write the word "Ending" on your Planning Sheet.
2. Write a sentence or two about the ending of your story.
3. Add to your story on your story sheet.

Sample Planning Sheet

ENDING

- The knight returns Princess Violet back to the castle. They have a fairy feast to celebrate.

Sample Story Ending

The knight rolled the big jar of honey off the fox. Felix opened his eyes. “Get away from me,” yelled the fox as he scrambled to his feet and ran away.

Princess Violet ran out of the fox’s den. “Oh, thank you, Ella,” she said.

“Let’s go back to the castle,” said the knight. “I don’t think Felix will be bothering the fairies again! We will have a fairy feast to celebrate.”

CHAPTER SIX

Happily Ever After

The last lines in your fairy tale are important. Most fairy tales end with the same two lines.

"And they lived happily ever after. The End."

ACTIVITY

A Final Look at Your Fairy Tale

Read your story aloud to hear how it sounds. Then ask yourself these questions:

- Did I begin with "Once upon a time"?
- Did I use a fairy tale setting?
- Did I include a title?
- Did I include a conflict between good and evil?
- Did I include a solution?
- Did I close with "And they lived happily ever after. The End."?
- Did I use correct grammar and spelling?

Think about the next fairy tale you want to write.

GLOSSARY

characters (KAR-ik-turz) people in a story

conflict (KAHN-flikt) a clash or disagreement between people

dialogue (DYE-uh-log) conversation in a story

evil (EE-vuhl) very bad and mean

fairy tales (FAIR-ee TAYLZ) fantasy stories set in a make-believe time and place

fantasies (FAN-tuh-seez) stories with magical characters or strange places or events

imagination (ih-maj-uh-NAY-shuhn) the ability to form pictures in your mind of things that are not real

moral (MOR-uhl) a lesson taught by a story

outsmart (out-SMART) to win out over someone else by being very clever

setting (SET-ing) the place where the events of a story happen

solution (suh-LOO-shuhn) the answer to a problem

villain (VIL-uhn) the bad person or evil character in a story

For More INFORMATION

BOOKS

Andersen, Hans Christian. *The Fairy Tales of Hans Christian Andersen*. New York, NY: Simon & Brown, 2011.

Ganeri, Anita. Fairy Tales. Chicago, IL: Heinemann, 2013.

WEBSITES

Fun English Games—Story Writing Game for Kids
www.funenglishgames.com/writinggames/story.html
Explore this site, which can help you write better stories.

INDEX

characters, 4, 8–11

conflict, 12–14, 16

creatures, 4

dialogue, 8

ending, 18–19, 20

evil characters, 4, 8, 12

fairy tales
- beginning, 10–11
- ending, 18–19, 20
- what they are, 4

fantasies, 4, 8

good characters, 4, 8, 12

"happily ever after," 20

hero, 12, 15. *See also* good characters

imagination, 4

magical powers, 4

moral, 18

"once upon a time," 4

setting, 5–7

solution, 16–17

three, 12

tricks, 16

villains, 12, 15. *See also* evil characters

About the AUTHORS

Cecilia Minden is the former director of the Language and Literacy Program at Harvard Graduate School of Education. She earned her doctorate from the University of Virginia. While at Harvard, Dr. Minden also taught several writing courses. Her research focused on early literacy skills and developing phonics curriculums. She is now a literacy consultant and the author of over 200 books for children. Dr. Minden lives with her family in McKinney, Texas. She enjoys helping students become interested in reading and writing.

Kate Roth has a doctorate from Harvard University in language and literacy and a master's degree from Columbia University Teachers College in curriculum and teaching. Her work focuses on writing instruction in the primary grades. She has taught kindergarten, first grade, and Reading Recovery. She has also instructed hundreds of teachers from around the world in early literacy practices. She lived with her husband and three children in China for many years, and now they live in Connecticut.